SCHIRMER'S LIBRARY
OF MUSICAL CLASSICS

Vol. 58

FELIX MENDELSSOHN-BARTHOLDY

Songs Without Words

For the Piano

Revised, Edited and Fingered,
and Prefaced by an "Appreciation" by
CONSTANTIN von STERNBERG

⊕

G. SCHIRMER, Inc.

DISTRIBUTED BY

HAL•LEONARD®

7777 W. BLUEMOUND RD. P.O. BOX 13819 MILWAUKEE, WI 53213

AN APPRECIATION

FELIX MENDELSSOHN-BARTHOLDY (1809-1847) is usually regarded as belonging to that Romantic School or period in musical history in which the names of Schumann and Chopin are of similar prominence. This customary classification of Mendelssohn, however, is not altogether just, inasmuch as it applies to one side only in the wide compass of his musical personality, and not even to its strongest side, for it emphasizes unduly that romanticism which was only an incidental feature in his manysided genius. The classification is somewhat unjust to Mendelssohn's other and far more pronounced characteristics; especially to those which so markedly differentiate him from his great contemporaries and which entitle him to be regarded as a "Classic-Romantic"—in fact, *the* Classic-Romantic.

While he could not—and evidently had no desire to—keep altogether aloof from the strong wave of romanticism that swept over Germany at the beginning of the nineteenth century, he came within its range only occasionally: when the text of a song called for it or the drama which he either introduced or enlivened with his music. Thus we find him almost transcendentally romantic in some of his Overtures (Fingal's Cave, Hebrides), also in his "Walpurgis Night," and above all in his music to Shakespeare's "Midsummernight's Dream," the elf-like texture and fairy-tale mood of which frequently—but also plainly—recur in some of his piano compositions (Scherzo a capriccio, Rondo capriccioso, and others).

And yet, when we enquire into the tendencies which were predominantly sympathetic to him and which he championed with all the strength of his personality, position and influence, we find them linked with the names of Bach and Beethoven. These were the masters for whose works he acted as an enthusiastic and energetic propagandist; it was their purity of form, their clarity of thought which impressed him far more strongly than the mysticism and fancy of the Romantics. With the farseeing eye of a divinely appointed prophet he perceived that these masters had spoken not for their time only but for all times, that their fundamentality would outlast every transient fashion; and it was in their path rather than with the Romantics that his genius compelled him to pursue his way.

That his works had lately to suffer somewhat from neglect is undoubtedly due to his so-called "followers," who—as usual with Epigones—had caught only the external qualities of his work (form, manner of workmanship, etc.), without its delightful and refined spirit; who imitated rather than followed him and who, by aping his style and by diluting his fine spirituality into a platitudinous conventionality, have wearied the music-lover. In the same degree, however, as these imitators fall more and more into oblivion (Sterndale Bennett is now completely forgotten), the true genius of their great model breaks forth anew in unimpeded light and reasserts its great, masterly qualities.

As the "Fugue" is inseparably linked with master John Sebastian's name, although his contrapuntal mastery was but one facet in the luminous jewel of his genius; as the term "Nocturne" is inalienably associated with the name of Chopin, though it represents the smallest type of his works and was used long before him by John Field—so has the "Song Without Words" become almost a synonym for the name Mendelssohn, not only because he—as far as we know—invented this original, paradoxical and yet so suitable title, but because in these wordless songs he has addressed his largest audiences. It is in them that he best conceals his great artistry and seems to speak the simple and intimate language of a dear old friend.

Open the pages of this unique volume wherever we may, the eye always meets a definite picture in the merely general aspect of the page. The writing is always decided and impeccable. The keenest search could not detect a page on which the master had not "something to say." Students as well as amateurs will find a perfect treasure trove of beauty and wholesome sentiment in this volume, especially if, in their selecting, they leave the beaten track of the half-dozen over-popular pieces in it and explore the almost untrodden ground of the many others. Varied as the sentiment and humor in them are and must be, there are certain features common to all: purity, chastity of concept, naturalness of melodic development with its consequent appealing quality, refinement of utterance, and, finally, a workmanship in the minutest detail that stands unexcelled to the present day.

CONSTANTIN von STERNBERG.

NOTE. Wherever it was possible to do so without making the reading needlessly difficult, the principle has been followed of indicating the use of the left hand by placing the fingering *under* the notes and for the right hand *over* them.

25496

Contents

Songs without Words

Lieder ohne Worte

Book I (Nos. 1 to 6), Op. 19
First published August 20, 1832

Revised, edited and fingered by
Constantin von Sternberg

F. Mendelssohn. Op. 19, No. 1

a)
b) } Imitation of the preceding melodic phrase in the r.h.

25496

25496

Regrets

Op. 19, No. 2

Andante espressivo (♪ = 120)

Ped. simile

Ped. simile

cresc.

dimin.

Ped. come sopra

Hunting-Song

Op. 19, No. 3

Confidence

F. Mendelssohn - Bartholdy. Op. 19, No. 4

Restlessness

Op. 19, No. 5

Venetian Boat-Song No.1

Op. **19**, No. 6

Songs without Words
Lieder ohne Worte
Book II (Nos. 7 to 12), Op. 30
First published in May, 1835

Op. 30, No. 1

Contemplation

Andante espressivo

7.
Composed
in 1834.

Unrest

Allegro molto

8.

a) The melody lies here in the notes which the thumb of the r.h. has to play; the characteristic figure of the (upper) accompaniment must be subordinated to it.

Consolation

F. Mendelssohn-Bartholdy. Op. 30, No. 3

Adagio non troppo (♩ = 58)

The Wanderer

Op. 30, No. 4

Agitato e con fuoco

10.
Composed
in 1834.

The Brook

Andante grazioso

Il basso sempre piano e leggierissimo

Op. 30, No. 5

11.
Composed
in 1833.

(legatissimo)

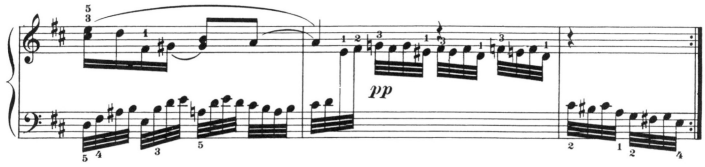

Venetian Boat-Song No. 2

Felix Mendelssohn, Op. 30, No. 6

Allegretto tranquillo

12.

Copyright, 1915, by G. Schirmer, Inc.

Songs without Words
Lieder ohne Worte
Book III (Nos. 13 to 18), Op. 38
First published in August, 1837

The Evening Star

Op. 38, No. 1

a) The slight curtailing of the third note of each triplet should be maintained also where this note accompanies a melody note, so that the latter may always outlast the former.

Lost Happiness

Allegro non troppo

Op. 38, No. 2

14.

The Poet's Harp

Presto e molto vivace

Op. 38, No. 3

15.

a) Small hands may play the lower E of the right hand with the left and change the fingering accordingly in these three chords

25496

Hope

Passion

Op. 38, No. 5

17.
Composed
in 1837.

Duet *)

Felix Mendelssohn-Bartholdy
Op. 38; No. 6

Andante con moto

*) The two melody-parts must always be distinctly marked.

Songs without Words

Lieder ohne Worte

Book IV (Nos. 19 to 24), Op. 53
First published in May, 1841

On the Seashore

Op. 53, No. 1

Andante con moto

19.

62

25496

The Fleecy Clouds

Allegro non troppo

con sentimento

Op. 53, No. 2

20.

a, Small hands may play the lower A flat of the right hand with the left.

Agitation

Op. 53, No. 3

Presto agitato

21.

a) This rhythmical reference to the theme should not be overlooked.

25496

Sadness of Soul

F. Mendelssohn-Bartholdy. Op. 53, No. 4

Folk-Song a)

Op. 53, No. 5

Allegro con fuoco

23.
Composed
in 1841.

a) The character of this Folk-Song has a strong tinge of patriotic sentiment. Introduced by a brief Prelude of violin character,
it is sung at first by a few voices which at every following stanza more and more singers join, until toward the end their num-
ber is swelled to a mighty chorus. Greatest economy of force in the first pages is therefore recommended

a) Small hands may use the notes in small type in the left hand instead of the bracketed notes in the right hand.

The Flight

Molto allegro, vivace

Op. 53, No. 6

24.
Composed
in 1841.

25496

Songs without Words
Lieder ohne Worte

Book V (Nos. 25 to 30), Op. 62
First published in April, 1844

Op. 62, No. 1

May Breezes

25.
Composed
in 1844.

Note: Play the 16th-notes with left hand where fingerings are set under notes; with right hand, when over notes.

The Departure

Op. 62, No. 2

Allegro con fuoco

26.
Composed
in 1843.

Copyright, 1915, by G. Schirmer, Inc.

Funeral March

F. Mendelssohn-Bartholdy. Op. 62, No. 3

a) It has become popularly known as a "Funeral March" because it was played —as orchestrated by Moscheles— at Mendelssohn's funeral.

25496

Copyright, 1915, by G. Schirmer, Inc.

a) These two figures may be played by both hands

25496

Morning Song

Allegro con anima

Op. 62, No. 4

28.
Composed
in 1843

Venetian Boat-Song No. 3

Op. 62, No. 5

29.

a) This remark by Mendelssohn means: "always with pedal", but of course not always with the same and continuous pedalling; it must be changed with every change of harmony, as usual.

Spring-Song

Allegretto grazioso ♩=88)

Op. 62, No. 6

30.
Composed
in 1842.

a) The letters *o.* and *u.* indicate where the left hand is best placed over (*o.*) and under (*u.*) the right.

Songs without Words
Lieder ohne Worte

Book VI (Nos. 31 to 36), Op. 67
First published in October, 1845

Meditation

Op. 67, No. 1

31.
Composed
in 1844.

a)
b) } Hands that are unable to stretch this ninth will do well to break or "roll" this interval *downward*, as it tends to preserve the
c) }　　　　　　　　　　　　　　　　　　　　　　　　　　　　　　　　unity of the melody.

Lost Illusions

Allegro leggiero

Op. 67, No. 2

32.
Composed
in 1839.

Song of the Pilgrim

Andante tranquillo

Op. 67, No. 3

33.
Composed
in 1845.

a) Small hands may omit the upper G of the left hand.

25496

Spinning-Song

Op. 67, No. 4

34.
Composed
in 1843.

Copyright, 1915, by G. Schirmer, Inc.

a) To avoid rhythmical angularity the increase of speed should not be made too noticeable. The following manner of execution is suggested at a) and at b)

25496

The Shepherd's Complaint

Op. 67, No. 5

35.
Composed in 1844.

*) Known as "Song of the heather" (Haidelied)

Lullaby

Op. 67, No. 6

a) In the first three measures the second and third beat should be played with a lightness amounting to a *gentle* staccato and this manner should be observed throughout the entire piece, but —of course—only in the accompaniment. The pedal is to be released promptly with the second beat.

25496

Songs without Words
Lieder ohne Worte

Book VII (Nos. 37 to 42), Op. 85
(No. 14 of the posthumous works)
First published in February, 1851

Op. 85, No. 1

Reverie

Andante espressivo

37.

The Adieu

Op. 85, No. 2

Allegro agitato

38.
Composed
in 1834.

Delirium

39.

Copyright, 1915, by G. Schirmer, Inc.

a) The accompaniment figure of three sixteenths should be played with great lightness and with special attention to making the last three sixteenths just be as light and short as the preceding two; it should *never* be held into the next beat.

b) This sign ∨ calls attention to the fact that an entirely new thought begins here — a second theme, as it were — and that the closing of the preceding phrase (on the first eighth) and the beginning of the new (on the second eighth) should be well separated.

c) as at b)

d(as at b)

e) as at b)

Elegy

Andante sostenuto

40.
Composed
in 1845.

The Return

41.
Composed
in 1845.

Copyright, 1915, by G. Schirmer, Inc.

Song of the Traveller

Allegretto con moto
sempre cantabile

Op. 85, No. 6

42.

Composed
in 1841.

a) The staccato of the accompaniment—to which the composer calls special attention by his remark "sempre staccato"—should be strictly maintained throughout, as it is to form a striking contrast to the easily flowing legato of the melody.

Copyright, 1915, by G. Schirmer, Inc.

Songs without Words
Lieder ohne Worte

Book VIII (Nos. 43 to 49), Op. 102
(No. 31 of the posthumous works)
First published in June, 1868

Homeless

Op. 102, No. 1

Andante, un poco agitato

a) Special attention should be given to the strict maintainance of this very original rhythm.

25496

Retrospection

Adagio

Op. 102, No. 2

44.

Presto

Tarantella

Op. 102, No. 3

45.

The Sighing Wind

Op. 102, No. 4

Un poco agitato, ma andante

46.

a) As the right hand has to play a part of the accompaniment in conjunction with the melody and as the prominence of the melody requires a heavier touch than the accompaniment, the differentiation of the two touches in the same hand calls for very thorough and special study. The changing of hands in the accompaniment should never be noticeable. Copyright, 1915, by G. Schirmer, Inc.

The Joyous Peasant

Op. 102, No. 5

Allegro vivace

a) A slight retarding, followed by a brief pause, is advisable here, to indicate that the close of the preceding phrase of four measures is at the same time the beginning of the new phrase.

Faith

Boat-Song

(Posthumous)

Op. **102**, No. **7**

Allegretto, non troppo

Copyright, 1915, by G. Schirmer, Inc.